T0196408

OUR OWN MINDS
CAN DECEIVE US...
People Do Too

TANYA CARPENTER

authorHOUSE®

AuthorHouse™
1663 Liberty Drive
Bloomington, IN 47403
www.authorhouse.com
Phone: 833-262-8899

Published by AuthorHouse 10/12/2020

ISBN: 978-1-6655-0327-3 (sc)
ISBN: 978-1-6655-0326-6 (e)

PART I

CHAPTER 1

Our Own Minds
Can Deceive Us

John 3:16 says, "That for God so loved the world, that He gave His only begotten son, that whosoever believeth in Him shall not perish, but have everlasting life."

Wow! How wonderful it is to know that we have a God who loves us this much. His Son's name is Jesus—the one who came down here to walk on this earth in the flesh, who was seated next to his father on the right side of him in spirit and glory, and who came and gave himself to be sacrificed so by his blood we could be saved from our sins. Now that's a deep situation. Can you even imagine giving up your son to save someone else? Truthfully, I can say I could not. That shows how much God really loves his people.

The sad part is how many of us on this earth do not know how much he loves us and that he created us and is the reason we wake up each day. There are a lot of people on this earth with their own theory of formulation, certain phenomena or principles of science as to why they exist and how they function each day. They are okay with this and not trying to seek the truth. Some go on each day knowing there is a God but not concerned about getting to know God. They know that God wakes them up every day and watches over them, and they are okay with that, not seeking to know that he is the same God who loves them unconditionally.

When we don't come to know God and his Son, Jesus Christ, we are in darkness, which means we are ignorant, without wisdom, knowledge, joy, peace, happiness, and strength—an easy target for Satan, who comes to kill, steal, and destroy us. The main thing he attacks is our minds by manipulating us with things that *look* good, but he just sets us up for failure. He tries to keep us from knowing God because once we do, he knows he is in trouble. He tries to make it like you've got it going on in your life with things like money, fashion, and cars, doing whatever you want to do with your life. Then come drugs, alcohol, prostitution, murder, rape, robbery, and many other things that only lead to destruction or death.

There is nothing better than knowing God; he never lies or misleads you. He is the only one who can save us. That is why he sent his Son, Jesus Christ—to save us from our sins and ourselves. We must go through his Son, Jesus, to get to God because Jesus knows what it is like to live here on earth. He walked here on earth for thirty-three years. He witnessed our pains, sorrows, weaknesses, and sins. Jesus speaks to his father for us because he came to understand what we go through while we are on this earth. No matter where we are in our lives right now, we need to know God loves us. He knows us, and he understands us. Sometimes we give up on ourselves before God gives up on us. He is the one with the power to deliver us out of any situation. God has the same power that raised his Son, Jesus, from the dead, and it's the same power that can raise us up from our mess.

Why would we want to stay in darkness, lost and not knowing what life is about? When we come to seek God and know him, we come into the light. God *is* light. His light is life with benefits and abundance. We must come to know the character, the knowledge, and the love of God. We must become new creatures of God. Doing so requires that we repent of our sins and ask God for his forgiveness. We can do this through prayer, as Romans 10:9–10 says:

> If thou shalt confess with thy mouth the Lord Jesus, and shalt believe in thine heart that God hath raised Him from the dead, thou shalt be saved.

For with the heart man believeth unto righteousness, and with the mouth confession is made unto salvation.

God forgive me for my sins. Come into my life to be my Lord and Savior. I believe Christ died for me. Give me the strength that I need to keep from sin.

When you have done these two things, you will have come into salvation, and you must believe that God has forgiven you right at that moment. There's no second-guessing it. We must come to believe that God really loves us. If you never felt love before in your life, please believe that God was loving you all the while. He has been there the whole time. It's just that we were not always looking for him. When we don't have God in our life, we go on feeling all alone, feeling like there's no way out, and feeling worn down.

I know because of my own life experiences while not having God in my life. But when we come to the point in life that we want to try God out, we read the scriptures from Romans, we say the prayer, and we are born again. We should get a new walk, a new talk, and a new look. We then come into God's kingdom of light.

I'm not saying that when we come to this new thing in life, we will no longer have problems. Sometimes we have more problems, because Satan gets mad when he knows he is about to lose someone who has been under his spell. When you come to know that Satan has no power over God, he can be defeated. When you get into God's Word—the Bible—and get on God's path, which is the road he has for you, you are lined up on one accord with God. Satan has no power over you. The opposite is true: you get the power over him.

When we are born again, it is a daily struggle. We must really stay in God's Word and do a lot of praying. Prayer is a powerful thing to retain in our lives. It's the way we build a relationship with God. My family and I lost my mother when she went home to be with our heavenly Father in March 2008. She came to me one morning in 2010. She asked me if I get down on my knees when I pray. I told her that I did sometimes, and she told me to get on my knees more. Now I get on my knees in the morning when God wakes me up and at the end of my day before I get into bed. I found that since I have been doing this, my prayers are stronger and have more feeling. I feel his presence with me. My prayers seem more effective. When I rise from my knees, I know without a doubt that my Father honored my prayers.

We must believe that our God is with us, loves us, and will bring us through whatever we must go through. When we come into God's kingdom of light, our new walk is to be renewed from our old ways. It's not going to happen overnight, because we didn't develop them overnight. We cannot change them on our own. We can only change with God's help. He can help us with change only when it's really in our heart. We can say we want to change or stop something in life. We can say it over and over, but it's just in our minds. We really mean it and are sincere about it when it comes from the heart. That's when God can do his thing. Amen.

God has a plan for all his people. He had each of our lives planned out before we were conceived in our mother's womb. He already knew who our parents were going to be. God loved us then, and we were already valuable to him. That's why God's Word says, "He will never forsake us." You best believe it!

When becoming new creatures in Christ, we learn a new talk. We learn a new language. I don't mean a foreign language, but it will seem that way because you talk a new talk with your walk. You learn to speak nicer words to people—even those people you couldn't stand, people who got on your last nerves. You begin to put dirty words away, such as curse words, nasty words, and hurtful words. You even learn how to speak nicely to your enemy. *Wow*, you may be thinking. I know, right? That is something. It's because you learn things God's way.

God is love, joy, peace, happiness, and truth. We become humble people. We look at life differently than people still in darkness do. I don't mean it comes easily, but with help from God, we can overcome it. We cannot and should not forget where we are coming from while God is delivering us. I must say there are quite a few of us who *call* ourselves Christians, but that's another story. While God is delivering us from our old mess, that's when we begin to have our own testimony. We can start sharing our story with those still in darkness and not be ashamed of what God has delivered us from. We shouldn't be ashamed to tell them about God because you better believe he is not ashamed of you. Each day that he blesses us with another day should be a day of seeking him diligently, first for his help and his strength to keep being renewed.

Now, Satan is going to be right around the corner. The first place he attacks is our minds. He comes with manipulation and lies. He plays games with you in your mind, such as, "You know you can't stop doing that," or "You know you've got to have that. What is it going to hurt?" or "You hear what she said to you? You better curse her out." Sometimes he will play on your self-esteem by telling you that you will never be as smart as you want to be, or you will never lose weight. We must learn how to rebuke him in the name of Jesus and tell him he is the liar that he is. Speak to him out loud and tell him to get away from you. We must learn who we are and stand on God's Word, knowing we have power over Satan. We must learn how to activate the power that we receive from God when we are in his will and in his obedience.

We cannot allow ourselves to get caught up in Satan's and other people's lies and drama. We have enough dealing with ourselves. Trying to do this new thing takes willpower, humility, and focus—being hearers, readers, and doers of the Word of God. Doing these things teaches us how to receive the joy, peace, and rest in God and in our lives. If we don't try to do this every day and night, it makes it easy for things to come and distract us. We can begin thinking that we are on the ball, that we've got everything covered and are on our way. A situation can come our way that we never had to deal with before. Then we will be lost. When we try to handle it ourselves, we will get frustrated, stressed, and confused. That's why we need God and his Word. He wants us to cast all our cares on him. You better learn that he can handle them better than we can. Our job is to continue working on removing old ways and habits—and even people—out of our lives. It's easy sometimes to let our minds deceive us. It can mean getting rid of old mindsets that hold us back from becoming the way God wants us to be, like Jesus Christ.

Accumulate wisdom, knowledge, and love. Second Corinthians says, "Therefore if any man be in Christ, He is a new creature: old things are passed away: behold all things are becoming new." Amen. When we are reborn, it's impossible for us not to change. We are saved by grace. Grace is a gift from God. When we are saved, first comes salvation. Jesus Christ paid that for us already. Then comes grace, which changes us. Grace justifies the sinner; it does not justify sin. That's where people get it mixed up. God forgives us but not if we are not sorry for our sins. Grace is the most amazing thing. By grace, we are changed. By faith, God comes to live in us to make a place for the Holy Spirit to dwell in us. It does not mean that we are already holy. God does not expect us to produce what we don't have. We must allow the Holy Spirit to take residency in us. It is placed in us to break the things in us that are not of God.

If we are a child of God, our souls must be broken. Our own ideals of ourselves are not going to make it. Our own minds can deceive us, and the self will fail every time.

First Peter 1:14 says, "As obedient children, not fashioning yourselves according to the former lusts in your ignorance."

First Peter 1:15 says, "But as He which hath called you is Holy, so be ye holy in all manner of conversation."

The Holy Spirit comes to change us and to help us be obedient to Jesus and holy. We need to take hold of Jesus and let him be everything he wants to be through us. If we let the Holy Spirit operate in us every day, we can get better and better each day. It can turn us into the person that God wants us to be in his kingdom, doing the works he wants us to do. God will equip us with what we need for what he has us do. He has everything we need to be changed and delivered from our old ways. When God's spirit comes in us, we are completely turned around. He also equips us to do what we are not used to doing. We learn to do things in the spirit and not in the flesh.

The Holy Spirit is always ready to help us, but we are not ready to surrender to the will of God. We must be rooted in God and his Word. The Holy Spirit must be released in us to bring out the gifts and talents God has placed in us. When we show that we are deeply rooted in God and his Word, we will have the urge to do his will, not our own will. There are wonderful things placed in every one of us by God.

We need to let go and let God. His Son, Jesus, and the Holy Spirit do what needs to be done in us to be renewed and do new things, to be an asset in God's kingdom right here on earth. We have a soul problem. We follow our mindset, our will, and our own crowd. Things like pride, selfishness, independence, and about one hundred other things need to be removed from us. So, let's now go into the different mindsets.

CHAPTER 2

The Mind

When we speak of the mind, we are talking about the intellectual or rational faculty in humans, the understanding, the intellect, the power that conceives, judges, and reasons. Also, the entire spiritual nature, the soul often in distinction from the body. By the mind of a person, we understand that which someone thinks, remembers, reasons, wills, perceives, and desires. A person can be fully persuaded in their own mind.

The mind is a polygraph.

Where the mind goes, we will follow.

Romans 11:34 says, "For who has known the mind of the Lord?"

The mind is an amazing thing.

The mind is a precious gift from God. He wants our minds to be peaceful, restful, strong-willed, and open to receiving new ideals. We can develop different mindsets due to our upbringing, and they can influence our outcomes in life, including our personality, attitude, and our character. We get stuck in our different mindsets, and it becomes the only way we know how to function in our lives. We can be deceived by our own minds, and it can keep us from prospering and becoming the best we can be. There are different mindsets, such as pride, selfishness, doubt, fear, worry, and unforgiving.

We cannot see ourselves unless we are revealed to ourselves. Then we should want to be changed to move forward in our life to be stronger and walk with confidence. The only one who can help us is God. We must want to seek him and learn how to pray to him for help to change. We cannot change or do anything in our own strength. All we need for him to help us is a willing and humble heart. God will not work with a person who has pride or a selfish spirit that is deeply rooted because they will be strong-minded without humility. The old saying goes, "A mind is a terrible thing to waste," and "Knowledge is power." It is true, but you must learn how to utilize them both to operate in them. Put them to work. If you do so only in the self, you limit yourself and prevent yourself from growing and knowing more, getting more out of life and God's kingdom. A person who seeks God and is humbled can grow more abundantly in wisdom, knowledge, and understanding and is willing to share these things and more with others. God loves a cheerful giver. He does not like when we moan and complain. The proud and selfish ones never seem happy or satisfied. They seem to have no peace within themselves. I'm not saying they don't believe in God, but maybe they first do as they want to do instead of what God has for them to do; they are not obedient to him. They want to please themselves, not God.

CHAPTER 3

Let's See Some Ways of a Selfish Mindset

Satan comes at you early in the morning. He starts getting all up in your head with a bunch of messiness to start your day. They're nothing but selfish thoughts. This can be a daily routine for selfish people. For example, *Nobody is going to ask me to do anything when I get downstairs today. He better not ask me to cook for him because he should have me some breakfast ready.*

Selfish people make everything all about them. They do not experience the good feeling that comes from doing something for others, giving you joy. They may stand alone in many situations because they're not humble enough to ask for help or advice. Even in giving, it doesn't come from the heart. It can be just because they feel like it, or someone else did it, so they will too. If they want to help someone, they want to call the shots and be in control. They like the feeling of someone needing them, but they will make the person wait until they are ready to do it. They can make a person feel uncomfortable on purpose. Also, they enjoy having the power to say no if they choose to. If a selfish person wants to donate some clothes, for instance, they will pull out their worst clothes, ones they had in a box for a long time. They wouldn't even think of washing them first before giving them away. From their perspective, they've done a great thing.

They want to do whatever they choose to a person, even if it's something they wouldn't want a person to do to them. They don't have a conscience about how bad they made a person feel. They're too proud to apologize. They can walk around every day saying, "What about me? What about me? No one is thinking about me." Murmuring and complaining is their thing. When things are going well in their lives, they are not concerned about others, even those in their circle. Their mindset is, *It's all about me.*

Selfish people will bring themselves only so close to God. It will be just enough to say, "I go to church." They only become churchgoers, not wanting to seek God for change because they don't see any wrong in themselves. They're not humble enough to listen to what God has to say to them. So, they can do as they please, not understanding how they are missing out on so many blessings that God has for them. Also, they don't see how miserable they are and how many people like them are lonely due to their own ways. Misery loves company, but life is too short for that.

A selfish Christian is caught up in themselves. Before they lend a hand to help someone, they say, "I will pray for you." Some of us forget where God has brought us from. They have their own clique of people they deal with in the church. If someone comes to visit the church looking dirty or smelling like liquor, instead of greeting them, they would rather talk about the person. They forget how they were once in their mess, and someone reached out to them. God said, some of our parents said, and grandparents said, "Treat people as you want to be treated."

Malachi 3:10 says, "Bring all the tithes into the storehouse, that there may be food in my house. And try me now in this." Says the Lord of hosts, "If I will not open for you the windows of heaven and pour out for you such blessings that there will not be room enough to receive it."

Oh, how we can easily miss out on God's blessings he has in store for us. The question is, Will we humble our hearts and minds to receive them?

Fear can also make people selfish, not wanting to do what's right because they feel like someone is getting something over on them, or they feel the right thing to do is the wrong thing to do. When someone lends a selfish person a hand, they are quick to criticize, showing no appreciation, and they can't whisper the words *thank you*. It hurts them to say it to a person, no matter how much they have helped them. They can easily forget what someone has done for them but are quick to cry about what someone has done to them. They forget what they have done to a person and don't give it a second thought.

At the end of the day, we don't have to give in to selfish people. We can treat and deal with them accordingly. We should pray for them to renew their minds and hearts, asking God to reveal themselves to them. Then they can see how others see them. Also, pray for them to become humbled to God and his will for them and not to miss out on what God has for them. Their purpose here on earth is to be a light for God's kingdom. Hope that they learn it's not all about them; it's about God and his Son, who is our savior Jesus Christ. He sacrificed himself for us, so, to be renewed, we must sacrifice ourselves for him and sometimes for others. We learn to be selfless instead of selfish. With selfish people, it can seem like early in the morning they got wound up like a robot by the devil, and all day long they say, "What about me? What about me?"

CHAPTER 4

A Mindset of Pride

The root of pride is self. Those who have a mindset of pride (spirit of pride) are motivated by self-righteousness. They do things their way without listening to reasoning. They will not admit to their wrong and will not say they are sorry to someone, regardless of who it may be, even family and friends. Proud people do not have a humble heart. They would rather suffer than stop being prideful, not realizing they set themselves up for destruction and failure because they are too deep in the self and don't listen to the voice of God. They are wide open for Satan to enter their minds and lead them down the road of no prosperity. Listening to their own voice leads them to thinking negatively and doubting themselves and others, allowing their own minds to deceive them. Having a proud mindset (spirit) will weaken your faith level because you are seeking yourself, not God.

Pride can destroy a person. A prideful person doesn't want to be obedient to God. They want what they want when they want it, no matter how they get it, even if it means stepping on someone else's toes. There is such a thing called sinful pride—those who make their own decisions without seeking God, thinking they have the position of power and authority. They make themselves the law or ruler of their own lives, which is dangerous to their souls.

Isaiah 5:21 says, "Woe to those who are wise in their own eyes, and prudent in their own sight!"

Prideful people can be lonely people. They push people away from them instead of people wanting to be around them because they don't take time to look at their ways and actions toward others. It takes God to reveal themselves to them. They won't like what they see. We can only pray for these types of people, hoping they realize their ways will not bring them good future. They will crumble. If they were to see themselves and want to change, it takes asking for God to renew their heart and mind, to walk in humility, to be able to hear the voice of God, reading his Word with a willing heart. No one can change another human or change themselves; only God can.

Let's understand that having pride is not a bad thing when it's about being proud of something you accomplished. It becomes a sin and ugly when you make it about the self and don't do anything that's motivated by love. If we encounter a person who has a proud mindset (spirit), it's best that we remove ourselves from their company and pray for a change in them. A proud spirit is a personality of Satan.

Luke 18:9 says, "To some who trusted in themselves that they were righteous and despised others."

Proud-spirited people can't receive correction or direction and won't ask God for help. So they are easily destroyed and fail without the help of God.

First Peter 5:5 says, "For God resists the proud but gives grace to the humble."

CHAPTER 5

Worry Mindset

Worrying is like a treadmill; it wears you out, and you get nowhere. Worrying doesn't do anyone any good. It is a waste of time. Worrying creates mental torment. Worry, stress, depression—these things come from Satan. The first place he attacks is our minds. He wants to keep us miserable and hates to see us happy. Worrying is totally useless and a complete waste of energy. Anxiety is worry. It robs us of today. We worry when we want things right now and it does not happen—something we can do nothing about. In our worrying, we think we can figure out our problems on our own.

First Peter 5:6–7 says, "Therefore, humble yourselves under the mighty hand of God that He may exalt you in due time. Casting all your care upon Him for He cares for you."

We need to seek God for all our situations, trusting and believing he has our back. Worrying is like telling God we don't trust or have faith in him. We can do it on our own. There is nothing too big or small for God. He is much bigger than any problem that comes our way. Our problems, troubles, and messes build our faith in God. What we go through in life tests us and builds belief and removes doubt in what God can do for us. We believe that whatever situations come to us, God can remove them. Our tests become our testimonies.

Worrying can cause stress, which brings on sickness, mentally and physically. Worrying comes from looking at the problems staring us in the face. Instead of praying or even shouting out to the Lord, "Help me," we rack our brains for how we are going to handle things. We need to spend more time with God and in his Word (Bible) to prevent our mind from worrying. Some of us get comfortable in our problems. That's when God needs to send a very big problem, and we must call on him. We have many sleepless nights and weep many tears when worrying. God does not like to see his people worry. He will send people across our path to help us and encourage us. Using them to uplift our spirit also helps strengthen their faith and ours (like a two-edged sword). We should make it a daily routine to seek God for wisdom for all matters in our lives, such as our spouse, children, jobs, health, relatives, and other responsibilities. It helps us keep peace and joy in whatever comes our way. A clouded mind can be a confused mind. You can't think or see clearly.

Romans 3:16–17 says, "Destruction and misery are in their way; and the way of peace they have not known."

A worried person is hard to get along with. Their mind is on their problems. They are afraid to take their mind off them, they feel like you are interrupting or don't want to help them out.

Worry focuses on ...

- 40 percent on things that will never happen
- 30 percent on the past, which can't be changed
- 12 percent on criticism
- 10 percent on health, which gets worse when we worry
- 8 percent on real problems we face in life

Worrying can be stopped by seeking God, the Word, praying, and reaching out to help others.

CHAPTER 6

Fear Mindset

Fear is the master spirit that the devil uses against us. He knows we won't make a move forward when we operate in fear. He likes to see us being fear-hearted and having a mindset of fear because he knows once we seek a glimpse of the light of God, it's all over for his manipulation. But we can't always give the devil credit. Sometimes we allow our own minds to deceive us. We stop ourselves the majority of the time, fearful of making a change. We hold on to our past hurts and pain, afraid to trust someone or ourselves. We don't realize sometimes we must change the people we hang out with, those who do not have an impact on our lives or are negative spirits. Not knowing God and his Word and promises keeps us in the fear mindset instead of rebuking the spirit of fear. When we fear, we can believe what Satan says and not God.

A lot of us fear situations like going to a doctor visit and hearing a bad result or losing a job, failing in a marriage or relationship, or even wanting to excel in life. We would rather settle for less. We look at the situation and are not willing to see beyond our problems, not knowing how to pray for God's help. We fear God is disappointed in us and our failure, so he won't answer our prayers. Without God, we will never be able to move forward because he gives strength, not the spirit of fear. Fear comes from our thoughts, our past, and Satan. It's his destiny to pull us back, keeping us in darkness. We can't move past the fear until we get to the root of it to be healed. If we get the mindset of saying, "I want to move forward in my life," and seek God for help and strength, we can begin removing the spirit of fear.

Matthew 11:28–30 says, "Come to me all you who labor, and are heavy laden, and I will give you rest. Take my yoke upon you and learn from me, for I am gentle and lowly in heart, and you will find rest for your soul. For my yoke is easy and my burden is light."

We need to seek God for all our fears, to replace them with faith and trust in him. God's Word says, "I will never leave you nor forsake you." We can look at our past problems and see that God had his hand in them all the while, because we are weak creatures in the flesh. So, when we come to God wholeheartedly, ready to surrender to him, casting all our cares, we begin to walk in the spirit with faith and belief. But even in the spirit, you can feel fear but not act in fear. Free from fear, you will no longer hurt people because you think they are out to hurt you. Learning to trust us in God and his Son, Jesus, will teach us to learn how to trust others again. Practice how to pray for peace, joy, and a sound mind.

Throughout my life, I have learned there is nothing better than peace of mind. If God is for me, who can be against me? Daily, we should pray for the renewing of our minds and hearts. To walk as strong men and women of Christ Jesus, not fearful of change, marriage, jobs, or building new relationships and having a forgiving heart for those who hurt us, including ourselves. Pray to God to heal us and restore us. Never fear what's going on in our world today. Know that in God's kingdom, we are covered by the blood of Jesus Christ. Walk fearless, knowing you are covered. Have peace of mind, not an evil conscience, which brings on fear. No longer allow fear to control your life. Do not look back, but look in front of you to receive all that God has for you. Be all that he has planned for your life. He will give us the tools we need to keep moving through our journey toward our destiny. Have wisdom and courage, knowledge and understanding. Stay prayed up; it builds our relationship with our heavenly Father.

Satan hates when we pray because he knows he will be revealed. He will no longer have power over you. When we come into God's kingdom, we learn that Satan is already defeated. With no more fear, we walk in confidence that we are the child of God and we have power over him. So, knowing this, we should know that God loves us, and we don't have to walk in fear in our lives. Live a joyful and happy life as God would want you to do.

Hebrew 13:6 says, "The Lord is my helper, I will not fear. What can man do to me?" God's perfect love chases out fear.

CHAPTER 7

Mindset of Unforgiveness

In life, we all have been hurt by someone who has deceived us, lied, put us down, cheated on us, or stolen from us. Some of us women have been mentally, physically, emotionally, and verbally abused by a man we loved and who we thought loved us. Some have been abandoned by parents and family members. Friends have turned a friend into the police. I know we can go on and on about how many ways we have been in pain and hurt by someone. The hardest thing for us to do is forgive them. We have the right not to be around some people. We don't have to torture ourselves trying to have a relationship with them that God didn't intend us to have. Some people bring friction in our lives. They don't want to see us happy.

The emotional debt is letting them control our lives. Then we go from loving them to not being able to stand the ground they walk on, wanting to do wrong back to them. When we attempt to, we as Christians feel convicted. That pain and hurt inside of us grows bigger. Our hearts can be hardened with no room for forgiveness. We feel we have been taken advantage of. We must know that even in a friendship, we don't have to be equal because some people don't know how to be a friend. They receive more than they give, so we must be careful who we choose and call our friends. As far as family goes, when they hurt us, we can forgive them also. Pray for them from afar. God's Word says, "We even have to forgive and love our enemies."

The only way to learn how to be healed and forgive is through God and his Word (Bible). Ephesians 45:32 says, "And be kind to one another, tenderhearted, forgiving one another; even as God in Christ forgave you."

Forgiveness does not mean that the people who hurt us win. Forgiving someone makes us free. If we have hurt someone, we must be man or woman enough to tell someone we are sorry and ask for their forgiveness. Not from our mind, but from our heart is the true forgiveness. Some of us are still walking around and living each day feeling guilty and condemned for what we have done or sins we have committed. We have not found the way to forgive ourselves. The only way to forgive ourselves is to seek God and read his Word, to learn how to repent and ask God for his forgiveness. If we do this, God forgives and remembers no more. He can teach us to forgive others and ourselves, to give us peace of mind and peace in our heart. He says, "He is our revenger. The battle is not ours; it's the Lord's."

We must be healed from our hurt and pain as well as freed from what we have done to others. Ask God to fill us with the Holy Spirit, that he may live in us so that we walk in love and kindness. Replace feeling hurt and angry all the time, not letting others love us and treat us like we deserve. We don't have to think that everyone is our enemy. Once we learn all this, when someone does come along and hurt or take advantage of us, we will know how to love, forgive, pray, and leave them in the hands of God.

CHAPTER 8

Mindset of the Flesh

The flesh is all over the place. It is weak, easily tempted. Being led and living by the flesh will always cause a person problems or lead to destruction. God's Word says, "We should be led by the spirit, not by the flesh." When we are part of the world, living in ways of the world. Satan loves that because we live in darkness, not knowing God and his goodness and his light, which sets us free from the dark world that Satan wants us to be in, to capture our soul to live in hell with him for eternity. Living by the flesh, we are easily drawn to temptation that leads to addictions such as sex, drugs, alcohol, gambling, and idolizing. These are a few of the many things that the flesh is weak to. Also, the mindset or the spirit of these ways is upon people who feel like there is no way out or no cure for them, because of not knowing God or seeking him for help. They don't know of his power, and he is the only one who can set them free.

There are other bad spirits not of God, like those who rape, kill, rob, and those who love to cause mental and physical pain to others. There is also the mindset or spirit of homosexuality and bisexuality. These spirits and ways are an abomination to God. But all of these are the ways of Satan's playground. Fornication is a major way of the world. It is in all our TV, books, and movies, even in so many of our young children. Our babies are having babies. Satan has us blinded to all these ways because he comes to steal, kill, and destroy with his lies, which is a setup to keep us lost and down in our lives and in darkness. It keeps us thinking that the way of the way of the world is okay, which is Satan's ways.

> Therefore be imitators of God as dear children. And walk in love as Christ also has loved us and given Himself for us and offering and a sacrifice to God for a sweet-smelling aroma. But fornication and all uncleanness or covetousness, let it not even be named among you, as is fitting for saints. Neither filthiness, nor foolish talking, nor coarse jesting which are not fitting, but rather giving of thanks. For this you know that no fornicator, unclean person, nor covetousness, who is an idolater, has any inheritance in the kingdom of Christ and God. Let no one deceive with empty words, for because of these things the wrath of God comes upon the sons of disobedience. Therefore, do not be partakers with them. For you were once darkness, but now you are light in the Lord. Walk as children of light. (Ephesians 5:1–8)

Scriptures tells us we should seek and believe in God and his Son, Jesus Christ, to be reborn, which means to be saved and baptized in the Father, Son, and Holy Spirit, to come in the kingdom of God, which is light. God gives us free will. He will not stop us in our choices … good or bad. But of course he wants us to make good and healthy choices for ourselves. We can take bad decisions as experiences in our lives to know what isn't good for us. We should not keep making the same bad decisions over and over, because we will be at a standstill, and no growth comes out of it. God still loves us in doing so. He's always waiting for us to look to him, for that is where our help comes from.

So, it's important to know that we cannot make it through this life in our own strength or our own wisdom and understanding. Wherever our mind is, we will follow. We should always think on positive things. When we are a part of the worldly life, which is living by the flesh, not by spirit, we can do just about anything. We are moved by thoughts, feelings, and emotions. We are without wisdom, knowledge, or understanding of anything we do. We try each day to make it on our own without God, who gives us all that and more to live, to have peace, joy, focus, and guidance in our lives.

When we get saved and come into God's kingdom, it does not mean we won't have challenges or temptations. In fact, it comes even more so because Satan is mad at us. He wants us to be blind and stay in darkness. But we learn that we have God on our side, and we look to him to fight our battles and protect us from the enemy. Living a saved life, we must learn how to have self-discipline and stay prayed up. God knows no one is perfect. That's why he gives us grace and mercy. Most of all, his unconditional love that he has for his children ... good or bad. When he wakes us up each day, he blesses us with another day to get our lives in order and to overcome circumstances. It's easy to get saved, but it's the walk in the kingdom of God that's hard. Without situations and trouble that comes our way, we will never know how to serve God or trust and believe in him. Circumstances come that build our faith in him, and we must learn how to let God love us, to know that he wants to bless us and not have us occupied, defending, and providing for ourselves. It's like a rat race that will not be won in doing it ourselves. We need to love and learn to seek and practice him being with us with open arms. Doing these things blesses God's heart. We should have a willing heart and mind to be humble to serve God. He wants us to love him more than we love anything or anybody. We love him by hearing and doing as Jesus Christ says, because he is all about the Father.

Matthew 10:37 says, "He who loves father or mother more than me is not worthy of me, and He who loves son or daughter more than me is not worthy of me."

Loving God is a different kind of love than loving our families. We love our families emotionally. God's love is through his Son, Jesus. It's being obedient to his Word, living by the commands of Christ, not to limit us but to liberate us. Jesus said, "The father passes all judgment unto me, and I'm not judging anyone." So, he is not sitting in heaven, waiting to hit someone on the head with a hammer. We can share this with the lost, but he said, "However, there is a judge for those who reject me and my word."

CHAPTER 9

Self-Discipline

Self-discipline is a sweet fruit of the spirit. Once we get saved to be reborn again to learn and come to know of God's love and grace for us, each day begins to be a struggle to become a new creature and renew our souls. We put away old things and ways we once were in the flesh, being in our sins. The love that God has for us, along with his goodness, helps us to not want to do the old things we did. There are some of us who said, "I'm never going to change because this is who I am." Of course, there are many today who feel that way. But when we come to God and his love, we learn we can change and break the bondage of our ways that holds us back from being the best person we can be, as God would have us be. The thing is we cannot change anything about ourselves without God's help and spirit. We are weak in the flesh. His help comes when we pray and call on him for help. It must come from our heart, not just our mind, to want to change or stop something in us, because God deals with us according to our hearts and our faith. We should want him to save us from ourselves. Only he can. He saves us from ourselves and death.

We all know of the old saying "practice makes perfect." It is a true statement. To become a new creature, to be renewed in heart, mind, body, and soul, we must want it first and then practice it each day. Change starts on the inside. God can touch each part of our flesh to be changed. He also can heal us from the depths of our souls, at the root of things that started at a young age, or that people may say were a curse from their family. Some people say that we can be burned with a certain spirit in us—for example, a spirit of homosexuality. Even so, this spirit can be removed with the help of God, but it must be dealt with as soon as it's noticed in a child or when one is confused as a young adult about what their sexuality may be.

We must always remember the flesh is weak. Even when we come to God to be saved, the devil gets mad at us because we are going to see the light of God and his Son, Jesus, and it is revealed to us that in his playground, we are in darkness. We learn we are slaves in sin and in the flesh. He only comes to kill, steal, and destroy us. So, getting saved is easy, but the walk is hard. That's why it's so important to seek God daily, stay in his Word (Bible), and pray as much as we need to, unto him and his Son, Jesus Christ, who sacrificed himself so that we can be saved from our sins and death. We need to work on self-discipline in our lives so that Jesus's sacrifice was not done in vain and to be the best people we can be, to let the light of God shine through us. To be people of purpose, good character, and of dignity. With God's help, we will change the way we walk and talk. Change can be a scary thing, but we must talk and think positively, letting it overpower the negative. Learn to stand firm and not fear. Know that we are not alone. God keeps his promises to all who call on him, no matter what mess we are in today that we need to be delivered from and the change we need in our lives.

Exodus 14:13–14 says, "Do not be afraid. Stand firm, and you will see the deliverance the Lord will bring you today. The Lord will fight for you, you need only to be still."

We must come to God for all our needs and to be changed. In all things we do, we need wisdom that comes from him. We need to be wise enough to know there is a change to be made in our lives, which is cause enough for us to work on being self-disciplined and using self-control in our daily living. When the storm comes our way, we can call on God for the strength we need to not react the old way. We learn not to deal with them in the flesh but in the spirit. He cannot and will not help a person with too much pride in themselves. We must come to him for help with a humble and willing heart.

A person walking in pride can be destroyed in anything they set out to do. Self can fail self. That's why it's so important to work on the self and believe in the self. You must pick up your own cross as Jesus did and follow him to crucify the old you and bring on the new you. Break the chain of bondage that had you caught up and messed up in your old ways. Change can be a wonderful thing, especially to come into God's love and goodness, which gives us peace, joy, wisdom, and a happy spirit. Why not be the best person we can be and be a good role model for our children, family, coworkers, and neighbors?

It is always great to share our testimony about how God changed us from who we once were. There are many of us struggling with the self. The thing is to want to change to be better, not to accept the ways and attitudes that can make us look ugly on the inside. We should want to build good characteristics. We can't change our circumstances, but we can change our attitude. We can deal with things with a negative or positive approach. Learn to deal with things maturely. Don't be frustrated when dealing with life, but have God's peace. It's always good to do God's will in our lives. He will give us all the fruits of the spirit to help us through.

CHAPTER 10

Why Should We Pray?

Prayer is like a vehicle that transports God's will from heaven to manifest on earth. Prayer builds a relationship between us and the Father. We should be giving him thanks when he opens our eyes to see another day. Pray before you get your day started.

Praying first thing in the morning can determine how our day will go. There is power in prayer. We need to learn how to bring all our situations to God in prayer, believing that God hears our prayers and that he will answer them. We should pray as though we already received what we are praying for. Prayer cannot work without having faith in the Father. If we're going to pray, why worry? If we're going to worry, why pray? Praying with faith will let you see the promises of God. The disciples asked Jesus to teach them how to pray. Then they understood the power of prayer. We can get our butts kicked by the devil without prayer in our lives because he hates when we pray to our Father. He knows we will learn how to use the power that God gives us, which is in his Word, the Bible. That's why it's so important to pick up his Word daily, to learn which scriptures to use each day.

> And take the helmet of salvation and the sword of the spirit, which is the word of God. Praying always with all prayer and supplication in the spirit being watchful to

this end with all perseverance and supplication for all the saints. (Ephesians 6:17–18)

Prayer is not something you do just on Sundays. Prayer is something we need to do daily. The Father wants to hear from his children every day, for us to know that he is real and is there for us whenever we need him, in everything we do. In this day and time, we need to pray for one another. Pray for the leaders of our nations and countries. Pray for those who don't know how to pray for themselves. We must learn how to pray effectively over our children, who can be swallowed up by the streets when dealing with peer pressure. Pray for our family members, neighbors, friends, and even our enemies. Pray for God's hand of protection for self and all the above.

God wants us to be specific in our prayers. We need to have prayer in our lives and ask God for forgiveness of our sins. Repent of our sins in prayer, on our knees. Some people have a prayer of petition is what a person need being specific in their prayer. Then comes maturity in prayer as we grow spiritually. We become more effective in our prayer life and begin to advance in the kingdom of God, where we can break generational curses and use the power of God to be seated in heavenly places.

We see wars on the news on television, but we need to know there is a bigger war going on, which is a spiritual war, a war between good and evil. We are the victims. The enemy comes against us in our finances, our health, and much more. That's why it is so important to stay prayed up daily in our lives, to always be under God's covering. In this world today, God needs a generation of believers who are not ashamed of the Gospel, those who love the Lord and will fight on their knees while God is fighting the battle for us. We can fight a good fight on our knees in prayer. We must know that we are warriors. We are marked, and the spirit of God is inside us. We need to know how to utilize his power in prayer. We need to be in the spirit. We cannot fight the devil alone.

One thing that edifies your soul is prayer. If we love someone, we pray for them. When we pray, we should believe that God will bring it to pass.

Here are some prayers for encouragement, protection, financial blessing, and thanking God for our family and friends.

1. Dear God, please give me the courage and grace to overcome the obstacles I face today. Please be glorified through me. Amen.

2. Dear God, protect me from anything that wasn't sent by you. Amen.

3. Dear God, please take care of my children. Protect them from danger and harm. Amen.

4. Dear God, touch my finances. I'm in need of a blessing that all my needs will be taken care of. Thank you for never leaving me or forsaking me. Amen.

5. Dear God, without you, I have nothing, and I am nothing. I need you every day, every moment, every second that I breathe. You are my joy and my strength. Thank you for loving me. I will praise your name forever. In Jesus's name. Amen.

6. Thank you, Jesus, for my life, my family, and friends. Most of all, you. Amen.

My Prayer for You

I pray that, for whoever is reading this, every ounce of fear, anxiety, and discouragement will be totally taken away from you. May God comfort you with his love and peace. May he refills your heart with his joy. In Jesus's name. Amen.

CHAPTER 11

Walk in Faith

Faith is a conviction, believing that God will do what he said he would do. God keeps his promise to his children. Worship produces faith. Faith gives you rest in a world that can wear you out. Keeping the faith in God will give you a happy spirit. A lot of us have something within us to be birthed. God is looking for people who don't give up! Keep the faith to reach your destiny. Sometimes it's not easy waiting to get there because we go through some tough times on the way. God knows where we are, and he will pull us through. When we walk in faith, we know he will never leave or forsake us. We should keep our eyes focused not on our situation but on God, because keeping our eyes on him will make what looks like a big problem look small.

God is working behind the scenes. With the help of the Holy Spirit, we can look forward to good things to come. Satan hates when we talk about faith. He knows that God has the power to help us whether we deserve it or not. God deals with us on our faith level. We need to use our faith to get wisdom and knowledge about God for him to use us for whatever our purpose is in this life.

Faith is trusting God with everything in our lives. He wants us to come to him for anything we need. He is bigger than our problems. Our faith is like jewels when we go through our trials. Untrialed faith is not knowing God's power. We grow by being tested in our faith. Having faith in people can hurt and fail you. Ask yourself, "Has God ever failed me?"

> Now faith is the substance of things hoped for, the evidence of things not seen. For by it the elders obtained a good testimony. By faith we understand that the worlds were framed by the word of God. So that the things which are seen were not made of things which are visible. (Hebrews 11:1–3)

Faith is a journey, not a guilt trip. So, get off that trip and continue with your journey. God knew we would slip to the left. That's why he gave us repentance, so we can keep moving toward our journey. We should never doubt the power of God. He created us, loves us, protects us, provides for us, blesses us, and forgives us. His love endures forever. Walk in faith and keep trusting in him. He is faithful to us!

PART II

CHAPTER 12

Deceived by People

When God created the earth and humans, he intended for his people to live in peace, joy, good health, happiness, and all the goodness he has for us. He did not say we would not come against hard and bad times while here on earth. In fact, one of the fruits of the spirit is mentioned in the book of Galatians, 5:22—long-suffering. It does not say how long we will suffer through something but to know that he is with us through it all. People have been through so much hurt, pain, disappointment, and deceit, torn down by people and the devil. Some even by religion and churches. There is nothing more painful and hurtful than to be deceived by family or your spouse, the one you trusted and planned to live the rest of your life with. In these days and times, there is so much hurt from children, parents, friends, and more.

It's not possible to get along with all people because some are led by Satan, not by God. There are people who live by self and self-righteousness. They do not know how to love or be loved because they have never known the love of God. Self can fail self. So how could they lead or teach another human? People can think they have it all together and be deceived by their own minds. Without God and his Word, we are lost souls walking on this earth. Satan has false lies and leadership. So we must be careful. We must have a relationship with God to know the tricks of the devil and other people. God needs to be present in every relationship to make it work. There should not be any room for the devil. You will have spiritual discernment and will know how to pray and fight together. There are so many single people in the world today because of different situations. It could be due to experience from a prior relationship, being raped, being a virgin and waiting on your spouse, doing it God's way, or just learning how to pray for patience to wait on the right person.

CHAPTER 13

Deceived in Marriage

God's Word says man should not be alone here on earth. Today, there are so many couples getting divorced. Marriage is when two become as one flesh in holy matrimony before God. It's a sacred and beautiful blessing for a man and a woman in God's eyes.

Proverbs 18:22 says, "He who finds a wife finds a good thing and obtains favor from the Lord."

A lot of us meet someone and get involved with them for the wrong reasons. It can be a lust thing, a sexual intention, the financial status of one, or simply what one can get from another that benefits their purpose. It seems that most do not take marriage seriously, or we just don't know the meaning or the importance of marriage. Nowadays, we shack up, become common-law husband and wife, and are in and out of many different relationships, not taking the time to get to know each other or build a friendship first, a foundation. In a relationship, there must be chemistry and compatibility, the same likes and dislikes. Most of all, you must have the same visions and goals to grow together and learn and build with each other.

One thing is true. The flesh is weak. So, we can be misled into committing fornication, which is a sin in God's eyes. In the world today, so many of us are deceived by the television, social media, magazines, and books. Having our children even adults who don't know God and his Word that are still in darkness. We are deceived, thinking that it's okay for two people of the same sex to be married or be in a relationship. God made Adam and Eve to be together, not Adam and Steve or Mary and Sue to be together. These things are an abomination in God's eyes. When two people meet, a man and a woman, they should be equally yoked under the same spirit of God, where they both know how to go to God together in prayer to let God be their guidance and strength. They allow God to be their third strand to hold them together. They do not let family or friends get into their relationships because it can cause more problems for them.

Communication, trust, loyalty, and honesty can hold a marriage together. Any relationship takes hard work and commitment, especially a marriage. It takes two to know what they want, and they must be ready to make a commitment to each other. Of course, it can be a scary thing to submit to another person. In this case, it is so important for both parties to have their own relationship with God. If not, it can be easy to stray from your partner, doing things that hurt and even winding up deceiving the other, committing adultery, thinking it's a way to make you happy or solves your needs.

It's very important for a man or a woman to know for sure that they are ready to share themselves and all they have with another human being, making sure that they got their play out of their system. A person needs to know how to love themselves first. Then they need to know how to love someone else and have peace and joy within the self. They need to willingly be ready to make that person feel special, wanted, and needed in their life. They should pray and fellowship together, making sure they both keep God as their guidance in their marriage, always uplifting and encouraging each other.

Sometimes in marriages, the husband can feel that he has failed his family, and the wife must pick up the slack. It does not mean she has lost her respect for her husband. The husband can feel weak as a man, allowing his mind to start deceiving him and looking at his wife another way, feeling envious toward her, not seeing that they are still as one together. Sometimes he can come to tears. That can even make him feel less like a man, but if she loves him, she will still see the man she married.

Washington Irving said, "There's a sacredness in tears. They are not the mark of weakness, but of power. They are messengers of overwhelming grief and of unspeakable love we may cry sometimes, but God will dry your tears. We may endure for a night, but joy comes in the morning light."

CHAPTER 14

Deceived by Religion / the Church

The Word of God says that we must be born again, each day becoming a new creature. Each day, the flesh dies and walks in the spirit. We pick up our own cross daily to carry. We become followers of the body of Jesus Christ.

Before God sent his Son, Jesus, to earth, we lived by the law. When Jesus walked the earth, we began to live by love and grace. Yes, we still lived by God's commandments. Through time, there have been many different religions created by humankind. Most have changed the Word of God's worship to their own God, to make their own laws to live by, which go against the Word of God. That comes with false preaching and teaching. That's why God's Word says we must pick up the Word of God for ourselves. Each leader is accountable for the leadership of the people. They will have to answer to God.

Some of us put our pastors, bishops, preachers, leaders, and the pope up on a pedestal as is they are our God. Some of our leaders lose focus of God and focus on self, money, and titles. Then, when the leaders are exposed for committing a crime, or a sin is revealed, the people are hurt and feel deceived. They do not remember that their leader is a man or woman first and is still in the flesh. They can still fail sometimes and make mistakes. These types of things make people turn away from going to church and believing in another leader in a church. Sometimes they stop believing that there is a God, calling Christians fakes and liars. There are some leaders who forget where God brought them from, condemning those who are not saved or born again, keeping their sins in their face. It's the same as religion does. Religion teaches you by law, the things we need to do. There's no passion or grace, keeping your wrongs in your face. They are ready to be judge and jury. Religion does not teach you that you can get help from God and that he's a loving and forgiving God.

When we come to Jesus and learn of his love, grace, and mercy, we want to change because of his goodness. There are some great men and women of God who are leaders over God's people. They and the church need to speak more and reach out to the communities to be witnesses of Christ, to tell people that God is real and he loves them. He is there for them in their needs, and he will never leave or forsake them. Our children were deceived by our schools when they removed prayer. Then came guns, rape, and violence.

Even though bad things happen, we cannot stay out of the house of God. Take the time to visit different churches until you find the one where you know the leader is being led by the Holy Spirit and not by the self. Pick up the Word of God (Bible) for yourself to learn the Word and that God loves you. All that He did for those in the Bible, he can do for you also. When you build your own relationship with God, you can't and won't be deceived by anyone. Some churches are still going on old traditions, and sometimes they don't have any growth or new members. God's Word says we must not stay with old traditions. The body should grow together as one. When we become a follower of Christ, we should not let ourselves be influenced by the things of the world. Allow God to be your guidance in all that you do.

Sometimes when leaders fall, we must forgive them as God would. It's your choice to move on to seek another church and leader. We should never stray away from God because he is the same yesterday, today, and tomorrow forever. We should never put people or things above him. When we keep that in mind, it can eliminate the chances of feeling deceived by those things. If we see things happening in the body of Christ, we should speak up in a wise manner. We should not let things go on in our churches that should not be going on. We don't always have to run. We must stand and work together as God would have us do. We must screen the people who enter our church to make sure we are not letting people become staff members without knowing their background. We need to teach our children that just because someone holds a title in the church, they can still do wrong to them.

Satan comes in many disguises. Some would say that Christian folks are the most hypocritical people in the church. They gossip and talk about people. For example, if a drunk person comes into the church, they are quick to talk about that person instead of welcoming them into the church. God said to come as you are. He wasn't talking to those who had it all together. He was talking to those who are lost and still in darkness. Church is not a place to judge others. Church is a place of healing, fellowship, and worshipping our God. It's supposed to be a place of teaching and learning, allowing the flow of God's love to touch everyone. No one is better than the next person.

CHAPTER 15

Deceived by Loved Ones / Friends

The most hurtful feeling is being deceived by a loved one or a friend that you trust with your life. We can sometimes put people before God, seeking them for our needs. We put them up on a pedestal, thinking they have all the answers to our problems, not realizing they might not have their own life in order. Those are the ones ready to give some type of advice quickly. Some will tell you the wrong things because of envy or jealousy, but in our eyes, they are perfect people.

Our own family members can be the ones to cause us pain and suffering. Sometimes they know they're doing it or believe that what they are doing to you is right, or they justify their wrongdoing. There are children today who feel deceived by their father or mother who left the home. Some end up in foster care homes. We must teach and learn that parenting does not come with a book. Sometimes, as parents, we can fail. But our God, he is our Father when we are fatherless and our mother when we are motherless. The best thing in life we can do for our children is to give them to God, making sure that we tell them and teach them who God is, as well as who his Son, Jesus Christ, is.

Love suffers long and is kind, love does not envy, love does not parade itself, is not puffed up; does not behave rudely, does not seek its own, is not provoked, thinks no evil, does not rejoice in iniquity, but rejoice in the truth, hears all things, believes all things, hopes all things, endures all things. (1 Corinthians 13:4–7)

If we do not know the Word of God and his love, we will never know how to love another. First and foremost, we must learn how to love ourselves. All relationships are important—marriage, family, and friendships. They should be made of love, trust, honesty, loyalty, and most of all communication. But somehow, some of us get lost along the way, with greed or thinking the grass is greener on the other side.

A lot of us had someone turn their back on us in one way or another. Some have snitched on a friend to save themselves from trouble. Some have been betrayed by a friend because of a business deal. Some have been deceived by a friend who cheated with their spouse. The list can go on and on. We must learn how to choose our friends wisely and carefully. Most of all, know the best friend who will never turn his back on us and will never let us down. His name is Jesus Christ, who gives us wisdom, knowledge, and understanding if we seek him.

The young and old need to make wiser decisions, especially when it comes to two people having a child together. It's unbelievable how many women use the child against a father who wants to be a part of his child's life. When it comes to a breakup, the mother keeps the child from the father, using the child as a toy to play with against the father, knowing how much he loves the child. They are called simple-minded women. The most terrible way to deceive a person is to hurt them. On the other side is a woman who has a child while in a relationship; she cheated but leads her partner to believe that the baby is his. For many years, you have heard about men having babies by another woman outside of his marriage or relationship. There is so much hurt and deceiving of one another in the world today. We take people and life for granted. There are so many of us who do not know how to trust because of being hurt or deceived by someone we were close to. We walk around with a steel wall up, not letting anyone in. We must learn how to be thoughtful of another human being, not to be so self-focused and selfish.

Everything we do should be for the glory of God, not self. There is no more being concerned about the next person's feelings or what they might be going through. No reaching out to the needy or sick because of being so self-righteous. No seeking God for change and growth. When we learn how to treat people as we want to be treated, we learn how to be thankful and not ungrateful. We must know how to live in these last days that are evil. We need to seek God and his Word daily to be saved and allow the Holy Spirit to live in us, to guide us. We need to have a good attitude to know how to respond and act toward people. God is thoughtful of us, and we should be thoughtful of where a person is. When we spend more time with God, we will change.

Ephesians 5:19 says, "Speaking to one another in psalms and hymns and spiritual songs, singing and making melody in your heart to the Lord."

We should take every opportunity in our life to be a good-hearted person, not thinking that someone is better than the next person and we can treat them any way we see fit. There is no blessing for a person with a cold or nasty attitude. We should have the mindset of "What would Jesus do?" God's Word says we must love one another as he loves us.

CHAPTER 16

Conclusion

The greatest gift that we have been given is life from our God, who created all things. He sent his only begotten Son, Jesus Christ, to be sacrificed so that whoever believes in him can and will be saved and will have everlasting life. We will never really know the suffering and sacrifice that was endured so that we could be saved from our sins and our ignorance. If we do not know or seek the one who created us, as well as the one who was sacrificed for us, we miss out on the blessings, peace, wisdom, joy, knowledge, and happiness that come with knowing, loving, and believing in our God and our Savior, Jesus Christ. Each day we are granted can be a day to grow nearer to them and to grow into all that God has for us to be, but we must be humble and with willing hearts.

Some of us had a start as a child; we were introduced to our heavenly Father and his Word. We went to church to fellowship and worship, giving God the glory and praising him. For some of us, it is in our later years. It's never too late when we are given another day to see, to be saved and come into the kingdom of God. Become renewed each day. Learn the characteristics of God.

We should also know our enemy, Satan, who comes to kill, steal, and destroy. Being under God's blessings and protection, we are easy targets for Satan. When we don't seek God and read his Word (Bible), we do not know how to use the power that we receive when we come into the kingdom of God and receive the Holy Spirit within us. Reading the Word of God will also teach us how to put on the whole armor of God each day, to withstand the wilds of the wicked. We cannot live in this world each day, walking around, not trying or willing to find our way to God. We will not survive in our own strength without any wisdom or knowledge of the true meaning of what life is supposed to be. We walk in darkness, without the light of God. Without the light of God, we will never know how to be healed from hurt and pain. We will not know how to forgive. If we don't know our God, we will not know that we don't have to be ashamed of our past when are reborn. God forgives us and can cleanse us to be new creatures. We learn how he loves us unconditionally, even in our mess.

It is easy to get saved, but the walk isn't. Our souls come with a cost. We must seek the strength of God to walk forward in love and forgiveness. God forgives us from our sins. Becoming disciples of Jesus Christ, we witness and share our testimonies of what God has done for us, how we were delivered from our past and sins. Not that we won't sin, but we know how to ask for forgiveness and repent of our sins.

No one is perfect. Learn to pray daily for strength, wisdom, and God's perfect peace, which he will give us when we ask for it. No one knows another person's walk with Christ. We all have a story to tell. When we learn the love of God, we learn how to be thoughtful and considerate of others. That's when we become selfless instead of selfish. There are those who have so much pride that they will never hear the voice of reason or God's voice. They can lead themselves to destruction and be destroyed because of lack of humility. When we walk in humility, we can be guided by the Holy Spirit, who helps us through situations and gives us wisdom. No one should want to be a fool and be misled by the tricks of the enemy.

We, those who are the followers of Christ, must know we have been given the power and authority of Satan. God has placed everything under our feet. When sickness, disease, stress, depression, fear, and worry strike us, we can put our feet over them because we are followers of Christ. When we have problems with family, friends, or other people, we learn that we don't wrestle against flesh and blood but against principalities, against powers. This is in Ephesians 6:12, "We are to love one another. Speaking to one another in psalms and hymns, and spiritual songs." But if we have not experienced the love of God, we will not know how to love ourselves or another person. He loves us unconditionally, no matter where we are in our lives today, whether good or bad. That's why we must seek him and his Word daily. His Word will give us guidance and encourage us to know all that he did for those in the Bible. He can do it for us. God has got us! Studying the Word of God can bring about conviction for you. It can show you when you're wrong. We need to stop letting people tell us where we are wrong. Let the Bible show you where you are wrong.

Studying God's Word can bring direction to for you. Many people can't get direction because they won't own up to conviction. Once you see where you are wrong, God can point you to individuals who can show how you are wrong. Then you learn how to do things right. Then the Word can bring about correction for you. Then you start marking changes to get it right. The only thing that will sustain us is the Word of God. When unfortunate things happen to you, only the Word of God will hold you. No social media, family, or friends can hold you. God and his Word will never fail you. In all things, we must be wise. Wisdom is from God. Godly wisdom is the master key that opens and unlocks all doors. It drives the power of determination. We should pray for wisdom to be able to properly judge, prioritize, and discern.

Many people lack wisdom, knowledge, and understanding of God and his Word because of their wrongdoing. They believe that God is mad at them and won't help or love them. God loves them anyway. They are deceived and tricked by Satan, and even their own minds can deceive them. They miss out on such wonderful love and blessings. No one is perfect—n matter what title they hold, how much money they have, or what position they are in. God loves us all the same. We should walk in humility with a willing heart to receive God, to hear his voice, and to be obedient. Allow him to guide us and to be under his protection. There are many benefits when you know, love, honor, trust, and believe with unshakable faith in our God. When we start learning and doing these things, we become new creatures in Christ. The old you will die every day as you put on a new walk and a new talk, walking in the spirit, not in the flesh. It's not all easy, but the new you will know that you do not walk alone now. God will be with you and live in you.

Matthew 6:33 says, "Seek first the kingdom of God and His righteousness and all things will be added unto you."

When you trust and believe in God and seek him and his Word daily, you have no room for fear or worries. Your faith will increase daily in him. You will learn that his Son, Jesus Christ, prays and speaks for us to the Father. He knows our sorrows because he came down to experience it in the flesh. No one can get to God, except through his Son, Jesus. He will never leave or forsake us. So, we need to give him the glory and praise that he deserves. Go into the house of God to fellowship and worship with other saints.

We should get tired of walking in our ways and self-righteousness. Self can fail self. When we do, we are open to destruction. Satan is waiting right around the corner to kill you, destroy you, and steal your soul. Why should we not allow God to do all that he wants to for us? He does not want to harm us. He only wants to bless us in our lives. For he is the one who gave us life in the first place. Don't give up or give in, no matter what the circumstances are in your life. Know that you can give it all up to God. He can handle it better than we can. Know that we are blessed by the best. No weapon formed against you shall prosper!

I pray that all who read this book will be encouraged and inspired. It is for all to know that they can live in peace and joy with all that God has for his people.
It's time to level up!
God bless everyone.

Printed in the United States
By Bookmasters